52 Ways *to a* Happier Life

Practical ideas you can use to create the life you were born to live

JIM DONOVAN

52 Ways *to a* Happier Life

Practical ideas you can use to create the life you were born to live

JIM DONOVAN

TREMENDOUS LIFE BOOKS.com

52 Ways to a Happier Life

Published by
Tremendous Life Books
206 West Allen Street
Mechanicsburg, PA 17055

Copyright © 2011 by Jim Donovan

ISBN: 978-1-936354-09-2

Printed in the United States of America

TABLE OF CONTENTS

Acknowledgments

My heartfelt thanks to my wife, Georgia, for her support of my dreams and vision.

To my Mastermind partner, Ski Swiatkowski, for challenging me to grow and for his endless encouragement.

Heartfelt thanks to Tracey Jones, Jason Liller, and the rest of the staff at Tremendous Life Books for their support of this book. You really are tremendous.

To Donna Eliassen at Viking Services and Denise Adelsberger at I'm Always Typing for their editorial and administrative assistance.

My fellow authors, speakers, and coaches who continue to share ideas to help us all grow and prosper.

I want to especially thank all the readers of my books and *Jim's Jems* newsletter who have provided me with encouragement and inspiration throughout the years. I am honored to have been a part of your lives.

Preface

My Road Back

There I was, living in a tiny bedroom in my parent's small apartment. I had run out of options. My life was out of control. I was one small step away from being homeless, living in Central Park in New York City. Years of rampant excess had brought me to my knees. I had lost everything and hit rock bottom.

I would lay awake at night, unable to sleep, pleading with God to help me. I prayed, begged, and bargained for my life to change.

I had done it all—been evicted from apartments, lived in cars, gone for days at a time without food, moved from place to place, and so on. Each time I told myself, "This time it will be different. This time I'll get it together."

I remember looking upward one day and saying, "Okay God, either take me or help me change." To be quite honest, at that moment, it didn't much matter to me which option He chose. That fateful day was many years ago, and my life has never been the same from that moment on.

Something in me wanted to live more than I wanted to die. So, swallowing my false pride, I accepted the help that was being offered and entered a treatment program. Upon release, I was on my path to recovery but I wanted more. I wanted the life I once had. I wanted the success that I knew existed, but had somehow eluded me for so many years.

It was during those days of early recovery that I read everything I could get my hands on. Frankly, I had little else to do.

At about the same time I was introduced to self-help books. This one small action changed my life forever. I devoured every self-help book I could find, listened to audio programs daily, and attended regular seminars. My life changed for the better and I achieved goals greater than any I had previously imagined.

After several years of immersing myself in this information, I began to write, mainly as my way of sharing what I had learned. Little did I know the impact this would have on my future. My writing, something that has always come easily to me, evolved into my books—*Handbook to a Happier Life* and *This is Your Life, Not a Dress Rehearsal.* Since then, these, and my other books, have been published in 22 countries. I've had the pleasure of speaking to hundreds of groups in seminars and regularly receive letters and email from people whose lives have been changed through my work.

As Og Mandino, one of the greatest self-help authors of all time and my role model, would have said, the hand of God reached directly into my life and changed my course from living in misery and despair to a life that is beyond my wildest expectation.

Today I understand that we all have the capacity for greatness. All we need to do is take responsibility for our lives, learn to dream again, set worthwhile goals, have faith, and take action. We will be shown the next step as our lives unfold.

Today I am totally committed to lifelong learning. I know that reading and listening to positive, uplifting information on a daily basis is what determines the difference between an exciting, meaningful life or the kind of life Henry David Thoreau was describing when he said, "The mass of men (and women) lead lives of quiet desperation."

to do. You are in conflict and probably not even aware of it.

Fortunately, there is a fairly simple solution to this dilemma. Begin your goal setting by first identifying what you do not want. I'm not suggesting for a second that you dwell on what you don't want in your life—that would be the wrong focus which could produce the wrong results—just that you devote some time and energy identifying everything you *don't* want.

In our business example above, you may have conflicting thoughts like, "I don't want more work, added overhead, more debt; I don't want to have to hire more people, and I don't want to work longer," and on and on.

By doing this simple step, you've cleared the way for the next important step: deciding what you *do* want. Once you're clear about what you do not want, with regard to your goal, you can begin to list what you do want to have and experience.

Again, in our example of "doubling your business," this might include such things as, "I want to double my business in the next twelve months. I want it to happen with ease and joy. I want to be able to do it with our present staff and budgets. I want it to be exciting and pleasurable for everyone. I want it to be fun and to have it occur effortlessly. I want to add more value to our clients. I want to explore new markets and create new ways to reach them."

Once you've identified what you don't want, don't keep going back to it. As a matter of fact, you might want to take your "don't want" list and burn it. Now devote all of your time, energy, resources, attention, and thoughts to what you do want.

By allowing your fears and concerns to become known to you, you've cleared the path for that which you desire and crave.

2

QUIETING YOUR INTERNAL CRITIC

If you read personal growth or self-help books, you've been taught to identify what you want to have. You've been instructed to focus your intention on what you want, because what you focus on is what you are more likely to achieve or receive. This idea was best expressed by the late Earl Nightingale who said, "Your mind moves in the direction of your currently dominant thoughts." This is an idea that can be traced back thousands of years.

Hold your attention on what you want to create in your life, since this is what you are more likely to achieve or receive. There is, however, tremendous value in looking at the other side of this equation, for it is in contrast that we find clarity. One of the blocks to having what we want in our lives is the internal resistance that is present and operating behind the scenes.

For example, let's suppose that you want to double your current level of business. I can hear some people right now gasping at the thought of that; however, it occurs all the time. This is one of the strategies I teach in seminars for people who want to experience quantum growth.

Here's the problem: you think "I want to double my business in the next twelve months." While you're focusing on this lofty goal, your mind offers some resistance to this idea. Your internal critic is chattering away telling you how difficult or impossible it will be, and even if it were possible, you would have to work twice as hard, and that's not something you want attended? What books have you read? What have you done for and with your family? What have you accomplished in your business? What about personal goals? What have you done for yourself? What about your health? Have you lost weight, begun exercising, or played a sport? Did you start a business, write a book, or give a speech?

Write down everything you can think of. Be sure to list even the seemingly small things. The more you list, the better. Seeing all you have done will raise your self-esteem and increase the likelihood that you will accomplish even more in the future. You have probably done much more than you realize, and writing it down will enable you to see just how much you have accomplished.

1

CONGRATULATE YOURSELF FOR WHAT YOU ALREADY ACCOMPLISHED

Several years ago, I began the practice of writing my accomplishments at the end of the year. I borrowed the idea from the corporate world. In most companies, managers are required to submit a list of their accomplishments and objectives annually. This information is used as the basis for performance reviews, raises, and promotions.

I thought, "If it works for them, maybe it will help me." The sense of personal satisfaction and encouragement I received after doing this once was so great that it has become a regular practice and something I look forward to doing at the start of each new year.

We take so much of what we do for granted, or just shrug it off, saying, "It's no big deal." We point to the successes, contributions, and accomplishments of others while overlooking all that we, ourselves, have done.

Only after taking the time to list our own accomplishments and activities do we see that we, too, are making a difference. We realize how much we have actually done in our lives, and this serves to encourage and motivate us to even greater heights.

In your journal, make a list of what you have done in the past year. Include everything you can think of. Where have you vacationed? What plays, movies, or concerts have you seen or

Today My Life Has Purpose.

Throughout the pages of this book, you will read some of the key principles that have helped me and countless others achieve the lives of our dreams. These same simple principles will also help you to live the life you were born to live; the kind of life that you will look forward to each day; a life that will amaze you with its magnificence. You deserve it, and you have within you the power to create it.

There are numerous ways in which this book can help you. You may wish to read the entire book from cover to cover, or perhaps a chapter each day.

However you choose to use it, be sure to complete the simple action steps and exercises, for this is what will cause change and growth to take place in your own life.

3

Balancing the Spiritual and the Material Worlds

One of the areas that creates conflict for many people, especially those who are on a spiritual path, is the imagined conflict between being spiritual and having an abundance of material possessions.

I say "imagined" because I do not believe there needs to be conflict. There was a time when I felt the way a lot of people feel about materialism, until I had a unique experience that taught me a valuable life lesson.

It was a wonderful weekend of lectures, meditation, and quiet walks through the woods, surrounded by more than a hundred spiritual people.

On Saturday morning, a small group of us stood outside the main building waiting for the conference leader, a deeply spiritual person. As his big, black limousine pulled into the driveway, I began to see the relationship between being spiritual and having an abundance of material possessions.

When he got out of the limo and stopped to play with the small children before going inside, I realized that while he didn't need the limo and surely never demanded one, when it was offered to him as a display of respect and admiration, he simply said "thank you." He did not say "No, I'm a spiritual person. I'll walk or take the bus." He simply saw it for what it was, a method of transportation—albeit a very nice one—and humbly accepted the gift. The powerful lesson in detachment was clear to me. We can enjoy material things without being attached to them. There is nothing unspiritual about wanting to enjoy the finer things in life and certainly nothing wrong with wanting to live a prosperous and abundant life.

As a matter of fact, it is the wealthy, prosperous individuals in any society who are also the ones making contributions to charities and non-profit groups, building businesses which provide jobs, and all in all, contributing a lot of good to our world.

So, do I enjoy material things in my life? You bet. Are they all that matter to me? Of course not. Remember it is the *worship* of money that is "evil," not the money itself.

"I have come that they may have life, and
that they may have it more abundantly"
(John 10:10).

4

WITHIN YOU IS THE POWER TO CHANGE YOUR LIFE

Success in business, relationships, spirituality, health, education, or money is the result of following a number of simple principles that have been passed down through the ages.

If you examine the core ideas in any self-help book, you will find principles that have been expressed for thousands of years. In my personal success library I have many great books dating back to the early 1900s. They all emphasize a similar message, which has become one of my core operating principles, "within you is the power to change your life."

Success is the result of practicing simple principles daily and progressing a little at a time until, one day, you reach your goal. Of course, at that time, you'll want to set an even bigger goal and keep the process going. It is our natural desire to grow in every area of our life. It is our nature to want to experience more of everything life has to offer. Wanting more loving relationships, better health, more spirituality and peace, more success, and yes, more money, is natural.

If you encounter someone offering to sell you the "easy secrets to a better life" or someone claiming to have "inside information for instant success," run the other way, because you have just encountered a twenty-first century version of the old "snake oil salesman."

Too many people today are looking for shortcuts. There are no shortcuts. Success is a matter of staying focused on what you want. If you follow the simple principles in this book, and others like it, you will reach your destination and live a life beyond your wildest dreams. I know this because I am living proof of the value of these ideas. My life today is delightful and continues to grow and expand. Believe in yourself, follow your heart, live your dreams, and remember the biggest secret—within you is the power to change your life.

5

Appreciate and Acknowledge the Abundance in Your Life

I realize that, for many people, affirming this can be a real challenge, however, it's really important if you want to improve your situation.

The keys to having more of what you want, whether it's more prosperity, health, time, fun, love, or anything else, is to first *acknowledge* that which you already have, and then to *share* it.

As you probably already know, we are much more likely to accomplish or receive what we focus upon or hold in our hearts. By "hold in our hearts," I'm referring to the feelings we have, for they, in addition to what we say, are what determine many of our experiences in life. Remember, "As a man (or woman) thinks in his heart, so he is."

By appreciating and *acknowledging*, for example, the health you already have, you are putting your attention on health, which is the only way to obtain it in greater measure. You cannot focus, as so many people do, on illness and obtain better health. It violates universal laws.

So your first exercise, should you choose to play, is to choose those areas in your life you'd like to improve. Health, of course, is a great place to begin, for without it everything else suffers.

You may also want to include love, career, and, yes, money, for they too are important. Ideally, we want to achieve a balanced life that is prosperous in all areas.

Take each heading and make a list of everything you appreciate about it as it stands now. This activity will align you with receiving more of the same.

After doing this in health, for example, you may notice you are making better food choices, exercising more, or making any number of other changes that will have a positive impact on your health.

When you begin to appreciate the wealth in your life, don't be surprised if you begin receiving more, sometimes from totally unexpected channels. I've stopped trying to understand just why this occurs. I just let it occur and give thanks.

The second part of the process is to *share* with others whatever it is you'd like more of in your own life. You'll soon discover that it is impossible to give without receiving.

If you want more love and affection, be more loving and affectionate to the people you encounter. I'm not suggesting you start hugging total strangers . . . maybe.

My friend, the late Charlie "Tremendous" Jones, made a habit of hugging everyone he met and it served him well throughout his life. Everyone I know loved Charlie.

It goes without saying that if you want more money, giving some away will help you receive more. I realize how difficult this may seem, especially if you're struggling to make ends meet, but give it a try anyway. You may be pleasantly amazed at what happens.

Even if you can only afford to give a little it will leave you feeling better about yourself and more prosperous. And, for sure, there are many, many charities and organizations that always need help.

Making a daily practice of writing what you appreciate in your life is a powerful activity that will produce astounding results, and it's something you can start right away.

Tonight, before you go to sleep, write five things you appreciate from the previous day. Do this for thirty days and then decide for yourself if it's something you want to continue. My guess is, once you start seeing the powerful changes taking place in your life, you'll want to make it a regular habit.

6

FOLLOW YOUR PASSION

No, this is not about relationships, although the principles will work in any area of your life. Recently, I found myself in a very strange state of mind. I felt stuck, kind of like I was walking through mud. I couldn't really put my finger on it, but something was definitely wrong.

As I began exploring what was taking place, I realized that I was drifting away from what I felt was my true calling and going in too many directions. I was, as they say, "chasing a paycheck instead of chasing my passion."

I found myself lured by opportunities because they looked profitable, when in my heart, I knew it was taking me away from my true purpose. The interesting thing is that when I've done this in the past, it has never really paid off. All I ever did was spin my wheels and waste time.

I decided to take some time and really look at what I was doing. When I do this, I always come back to writing and speaking as my true purpose. I believe God pulled me from the depths of despair and a life of misery and degradation, so that I could use what I have learned to help others, and my books and seminars are one of the ways I am to do that.

When I made that decision and reconfirmed my commitment to my true purpose and passion, interesting things happened.

Doors opened and I started receiving inquiries about delivering seminars. One area that I felt guided to focus on is delivering talks to students and their parents. I feel strongly that our young people need to hear more uplifting messages, and I feel that I can help. Interestingly enough, as soon as I decided this, I received an invitation to speak at a high school.

What is the passion you're distracted from? Maybe it's your relationships. Have you been less than fully committed, choosing instead to just coast along, expecting it to take care of itself without input from you?

What about your career or business? Do you still have the passion you had when you began, or have you become complacent, just going through the motions? Have you abandoned your passion, thinking success is somewhere else?

Don't be like the man in the story *Acres of Diamonds*, written by Russell Conwell. In this classic story, a man left his farm in search of diamonds and spent years in search of them, only to end up destitute. The person who bought the farm from him discovered the diamonds right on the man's property. Sometimes we have to look, literally, in our own backyards.

Action Step: Renew Your Passion.

What is your passion? What have you always felt strongly about?

Why did you want this in the first place? What drove you?

How does doing this make you feel?

How can you reconnect with your passion?

What can you do now to get going again?

7

What Do You Love to Do?

Some of the wealthiest and most successful individuals in the world are known to make statements like, "I'm having so much fun; I can't believe I get paid for this." This type of sentiment reflects what it feels like to express your natural gifts and do work that you are absolutely passionate about. People often ask me how they can find their "purpose" or what business they should start. The "secret" is in the quotation expressed above.

Find whatever it is that you do naturally, without thinking about it. What would you do even if you were not being paid for it? For me this is writing and speaking, essentially variations on a theme of being able to communicate information that will help other people. It's something that I just do, something that I started doing years before I ever thought about making a living at it. I began writing a newsletter several years before I even considered writing a book and way before I began doing seminars.

Action Step: Finding Your Passion.

What is it that you've always been good at?

What is it that you do just because you enjoy doing it?

What would you do if money did not matter?

The answers to these questions will guide you towards your true calling, your passion. You owe it to yourself to explore these ideas and follow your bliss. It may not happen overnight; it rarely does. But if you're persistent and keep following your internal guidance and intuition, you may be one of those fortunate people who can honestly say, "I would do this even if I didn't get paid for it."

8

ARE YOU SETTLING FOR SMALL GOALS?

Recently, during a multipart workshop I delivered for a local business, we had a discussion about goals. Goals and goal setting have been major components of my work for the past two decades. Goal setting is the single most important skill I learned that enabled me to change my own life.

Setting goals, visualizing their achievement, and of course, taking action, have enabled me to transform my life and create a life that is beyond anything I could have expected back when I was just trying to get to the point of survival, much less success.

It has been my practice of setting goals—usually at the start of the year and then again on my birthday in June—that has contributed to everything I now enjoy in my life. I once read that if you can become clear about what you want for the coming year, on your birthday, you can achieve it. While any time is a good time to get started designing your life the way you desire it, your birthday is the most powerful day of your year. I typically make revisions at the start of the New Year since, in my case, it's the halfway point.

What I learned in our discussion was that many people in the group had a habit of setting goals they knew they could easily achieve. The reasoning was that to do anything else would mean that they might not make it, and in their eyes, this represented failure.

This totally floored me and led to a lengthy discussion

about goals and redefining failure. For me personally, I cannot fail unless I give up, and I'm not about to do that. Years ago, I learned the concept of making failure impossible and success easy to achieve.

By making it easy to experience the feelings of success, you make it that much easier to motivate yourself to continue.

Setting a goal that you know you can achieve, to me, is a big yawn. This may be fine for the day-to-day things in your life, like a goal to walk four days a week. But is this really a goal, or is it just a task?

Your important goals should, at the same time, excite and challenge you.

As I said earlier, the problem some of the people in the group had was feeling that if they fell short of their goal, they had failed. Like most things in life, that's really just a perception. I've always liked the idea Les Brown expressed when he said "If you reach for the moon and miss, you still have the stars." Personally, I'd rather fall a little short of a huge goal than achieve a small one.

While small goals are helpful and may even be measurable milestones on your way to a bigger goal, I feel the things that matter in my life deserve a grander vision.

If I set a goal, as I did recently, to reach a weight that is 24 pounds less than what I am now by a certain date, and only lose twenty pounds, have I failed? Certainly not. If you set a goal to earn $250,000 in the next twelve months and only earn $225,000, have you failed? Not likely.

Chances are if the goal was really a stretch, you were making $100,000 or less when you set it. Though you missed your target, you still more than doubled your income and that's a huge accomplishment in anyone's book.

Action Step: Please Answer the Following:

If you knew you would not fail, what great dream would you attempt?

What one action will you take in the next 24 hours to begin moving toward it?

9

How Exciting Are Your Goals?

Written goals will change your life. I guarantee it! Spend some time thinking about what you'd like your life to be like. For the sake of this exercise, let's set goals you'd like to have accomplished one year from now. Of course, you can set shorter and longer goals as well.

What would you like for your relationships? What about your health, career, and, finances? What about your educational, social, and material goals? What would you like to experience? What would you like to do, be, and have? Invest some time now to identify these things and write them down. This will greatly increase the likelihood of accomplishing them. Do your goals make you want to jump out of bed each day, eager to get going?

In their careers, many people tend to look at the next step on their path. As I said earlier, this is fine and will help you achieve your next promotion but how exciting is it? What if, instead of looking at your next milestone, you focused on your ultimate goal within your company?

If you're a salesperson, a goal of steadily reaching your quota may be your logical next step, but how much more exciting would it be to awaken in the morning knowing that you would soon be the top producer in your entire organization?

When I was barely nineteen years old, I took a position as a door-to-door salesman selling vacuum cleaners. I had been told that I was too young and, never being one to let age stop me, I challenged the manager. I said that I would be the top salesperson in the office my first month. I'm not sure why I said that, not having any sales experience to speak of, but I guess I didn't like being told that I could not do something. The top producers each month were honored with a small trophy and sat on a dais with the other top producers from around the region at the monthly banquet.

Not even knowing what a goal was, I had set one. Though I understood little about the power of my subconscious mind, I started seeing myself on the stage receiving the trophy. For me it was not how many vacuums I would sell or even the commissions that I would earn. I wanted the trophy! At my young age this was enough to get me jumping out of bed each day, doing my best all day, and working into the evening hours, long after everyone else had quit.

At any age, having a goal that is bigger than you will spark your creativity and get you moving in the direction of your dreams. At the luncheon that month, I sat on the dais with some of the top producers in the company, proudly holding my trophy.

Set goals that are beyond your reach. Goals that are huge enough to really get you excited. Then, when you think about your new, bigger goals, you'll get excited just imagining what it would feel like reaching them and what your life would be like having accomplished them. And even if you don't fully reach them, you will have progressed beyond what you might have accomplished, plus you will feel better during the process.

10

WHY DO YOU WANT IT?

If you've completed the previous exercise, congratulations. If not, please go back and do it now. Goal setting is one of the absolute keys to enjoying a successful life.

Your goals list most likely includes things like, "a better relationship with my spouse or children; peace of mind; to be happy; a better job; my own business; a new car or house; a college degree; a vacation," or everyone's favorite, "*more money.*" If I were to ask you *why* you wanted these things, could you tell me? In seminars, I often hear people say they want more money, but when pressed as to "why," they draw a blank.

It has been said that we can accomplish anything if we have a big enough reason. When asked why she did what she did, the late Mother Teresa replied, "So that all people can die with dignity." Her "why" was so powerful a motivator for her that this small, saintly woman was able to create a massive, worldwide community that continues to help the poor, sick, and dying long after her death.

What are your "whys?" For example, if you, like most people, want more money, why do you want it? What does it mean to you? What will it do for you? Will it give you security, freedom, happiness, or some other "result" that is important to you? How will having more money make you feel? The more you can focus on the "why" of your goals and the "feelings" they will produce, the more you will be motivated to act, and the faster you will draw it to you.

Action Step: Why You Want Your Goals.

1. Make a list of your top four or five one-year (or longer) goals. Next to each, list as many reasons as you can think of for wanting this goal.

2. List the powerful, positive feelings you will experience when you have reached this goal.

Devote some time each day to visualizing yourself as having reached your goal, and try to imagine how you will feel when you reach it. Feeling the feelings will place you in a better position to accomplish what you want.

11

ARE YOUR GOALS WORTHY?

The other day while I was delivering an all-day workshop to a group of managers, one of the participants asked a great question. I had gone through the process of identifying what your ideal life would look like, creating a compelling vision for your future, and extracting specific goals towards its achievement. So far, so good.

During a segment about values, and what it would take for one to feel successful, I suggested making it easy to experience success, and difficult, if not impossible, to feel failure.

For me, failure means giving up. Anything else is simply a temporary setback and usually a great learning experience.

A woman asked, "How do you explain the two? Seeing a clear vision of your ideal life, while at the same time feeling content with where you are."

What a great question.

Earl Nightingale, one of the earliest personal development teachers and co-founder of Nightingale-Conant, defined success as "The progressive realization of a worthy ideal."

For me, this is the key. The operative word here is "progressive." As long as I am progressing toward a vision that I feel is worthy, I am succeeding.

It's the journey, not the destination, that makes it all worthwhile. I once heard a personal development teacher beautifully point out that the word *worthy* refers to the goal being worth *your* time and energy.

In other words, it's not about what you get that makes it

worthy, it's a question of whether the goal is worthy of you taking the time out of your life to pursue it. Think about that.

Are Your Goals Worthy of Your Life?

Many people have a tendency to set small goals. If you consider that the price of any achievement is your time and that your time is all you really have that is of real value, you will soon see the importance of having a vision that is worthy of expending your life's energy upon it.

A great activity is to go back over your goals and see if they meet the criteria of being worthy of you, not the other way around. If not, maybe you want to stretch yourself and go for something more important to you. Whatever you achieve, you are paying with the time of your life. Make sure it's worth the asking price.

12

Fuzzy Goals Just Won't Do

The more clearly you know what you want, the more likely it is you will have it.

The young woman in my workshop said, "I want a new house!"

"What type of house do you want? Where do you want to live?" I asked.

"I don't care. I just want my own house," she replied.

What do you think the chances are that the house will manifest? If you said "slim," you are right. If I were on a special assignment with all the resources necessary to bless her with anything she wanted and she replied the way she did, I would say, "When you figure out what you want, let me know and I will deliver it to you." Then I would walk away in frustration.

If your child came to you and asked for a toy, you would probably ask, "What kind?" And then do your best to give it to her or him. We are God's children and He wants to give us what we ask for, but … we have to ask!

The clearer you are about what you want, the more descriptive and detailed your desire, the easier it will be to see it manifested. In my seminars, I teach people that if they want a car, for example, to be specific about the type, model, and color, and provide as much detail as possible.

To engage other senses, especially for material things like cars, I suggest getting a photo of the item and putting it where it will be seen. Better yet, go to a dealership and ask a salesperson to take a picture of you sitting in the car of your dreams.

This is the same as making a "dream board" or "treasure map," something I have been using and teaching for years.

If it's a special relationship that you want to attain, make a list of the chief characteristics and traits of your ideal partner. In your business, you can use this same idea and list the characteristics of your perfect customer.

Once you become clear as to exactly what you want, you move on to the "asking part." The Bible says, "ask and it shall be given." Notice that it does not say, "beg or whine."

An ideal way to ask is by using affirmative prayer, a technique that is taught by some of the credible spiritual leaders of our time. It is the concept of giving thanks as if you have already received what you desire by using an affirmative prayer such as "I give thanks that my financial situation is improving dramatically because I am blessed by the God who created heaven and earth," or, "Thank you, God, for the abundant health I now enjoy."

By invoking affirmative prayer, you are giving thanks and affirming your belief that what you asked for is in fact given unto you.

The Simple Process Is:

• Identify what you want in as much detail as possible.

• Be thankful for having received it.

• Remain open to allowing it to come to you.

• Act on whatever inspiration you receive

13

DON'T PUSH YOUR GOALS AWAY

You're probably asking yourself, "Why would anyone want to push his or her goals away?" After all, our goals represent what we want in our lives, right? It would seem so, but in reality we often set ourselves up to fail every time we think about a goal or even just something we want to have or do in our lives.

Colleen thinks to herself, "I would really like to own my own home-based business" (the goal). Then, instead of basking in the good feelings associated with that worthy ideal, the very next thought that comes into her mind is "How will I ever do it? I have to take care of the kids and all." She has literally pushed the goal away in her mind even before it had a chance to settle in.

Wayne thinks, "I'd really like to drop a few pounds and get in better shape" (the goal). Then, before he gives himself a chance to achieve the goal, he thinks, "That will be hard and will take up even more of my time. I don't have enough time as it is now."

The two cases above are typical examples of how we often push our goals away, usually before they even have time to develop. You think to yourself, "I'd like a new car." The very next thought is, "That's ridiculous! I can't even afford the car I have now. How can I get a new car?"

If you want to live a wonderful life, achieving your goals and being able to enjoy what you want in your life, you must first change this "knee-jerk" reaction. We all do this to some extent, at least until we become aware of it and start taking specific actions to change it.

Whenever the little voice in your mind rears its ugly head, tell it to sit down and be quiet. You must silence the negative, limiting thoughts in your mind. Even if your goal is totally outrageous, you must remain open to the possibilities of achieving it if you intend to succeed. There will be plenty of time for a "reality check" later.

One of the ways you can start overriding your destructive self-talk is to create two or three positive affirmations that will help you attain whatever it is you want. For example, in the case of getting in better physical condition, you might start affirming, "Every day, I am becoming healthier and healthier." You could add to that, "I am enjoying my exercise time and making healthier food choices."

It's important, when creating affirmations, to make sure they are positive and in the present tense. Saying "I will be . . ." will cause your subconscious mind to keep your goal out in front of you. Remember, your subconscious mind does not know the difference between what is real and what is vividly imagined. This is one of the reasons Olympic athletes and other sports figures have been able to effectively use visualization to enhance their training. A swimmer, for example, who vividly imagines the race will be sending messages to her body, and the associated muscles will be firing.

Making sure your affirmations are stated in the positive is equally important, since your subconscious mind does not recognize negatives. If I ask you not to think of a purple kangaroo, what happens? Exactly.

See Your Ideal Life

In addition to reading and reciting your affirmations, devote some time each day to visualizing your life as you would like it to be. This need not take a long time. Usually ten or fifteen minutes are sufficient. See your goal as having already occurred and see yourself enjoying your ideal life. Really get into it. Engage all your senses—sound, taste, touch, color, etc. If you want a home near the ocean, hear the sound of the breaking waves. Smell the salt air. You have the idea.

14

AFFIRMATIONS

Hopefully, you've stretched yourself and identified some of the things that would make you say, "Wow! This is great."

Now I'd like you to go back over your "dreams" list and pick one or two things you wrote for each area of your life. Ideally, you have a couple of desires for your health, your work or business, your family and leisure time, material things, social activities, spiritual pursuits, and, of course, finances.

If you're doing this for your business, you may have listed your ideal level of sales and income, new product creation, growth, new clients, employee performance, and so on.

For each of these, create a goal in the form of a positive affirmation. For example, for your health you could write, "I am so happy I'm at my ideal weight of ____ pounds and feel great." Be sure to include a measurable number.

If this stirs up some resistance or disbelief, here is a tip I learned that might prove to be helpful to you. Use a "bridge" statement like, "I'm in the process of . . . ." in front of your affirmation.

This takes away any internal resistance you may have that is preventing you from reaching your goal.

Create a positive affirmation—which you can believe—for each of your goal statements. You may want to use the SMART method: make each goal Specific, Measurable, Actionable, Realistic, and Timed.

My only challenge to this is the idea that a goal needs to

be "realistic." I feel it's more important that your goal be "believable" than realistic. (Unfortunately, SMABT does not spell anything!)

Since reality, in essence, is something we are creating by our thoughts, it doesn't really matter how realistic something is to someone else. However, you will never reach a goal you do not *believe* can be accomplished.

This is why so many people do not reach their goals. They are internally conflicted between what they *say* they want and what they *believe* they can achieve.

One simple way to move through this is to use one of the "bridge" statements to lessen your resistance. By adding the bridge to your affirmations, they become more "believable" to your mind.

The obvious next step, which most people do after setting their goals, is to create an action plan, listing the steps they'll take to reach their destinations; however, I want to add one small but powerful step in between.

I'd like you to imagine you've already reached all your goals and are enjoying the life you've created. Really step into this. Engage all your senses and put yourself in that energy of completion.

You may choose to write this out into a one- or two-page vision statement that you can use daily to get into the energy of having reached your goals. I've been doing this for several years and it's made a huge difference in my life.

Whether you write out your vision or not, be sure to invest some time each day to get into the *feeling* of having achieved your desires. The more you do this, the faster you will manifest it in your life.

15

SURRENDER AND WIN

I believe that surrendering to God is another one of those "keys" to helping us through whatever we're facing. Whether your present challenge is related to health, business, or career, or for that matter anything else, surrendering to the idea of a solution from outside your normal realm of thought is a sure way out. Our tendency is to hang on, attempting to find a solution, when in fact the opposite approach often yields the result we want.

Don't confuse "surrender" with giving up. It's quite the opposite. Surrendering is realizing that, alone, we accomplish little or nothing. By surrendering to a power greater than ourselves, we make available the help that has always been there for us.

By surrendering, we release the tension that is causing us stress, constricting our blood vessels, and probably impeding our brain's ability to think clearly. By surrendering we open ourselves up to the guidance that is always available to us. Of course, we still have our part to play in this process.

Action Step: Learning to Let Go

The next time you're faced with a challenge, try this surrender exercise:

1) Define the challenge clearly.

2) Write it down.

3) If possible, put it away for at least 24 hours.

4) Ask for help. Just sit quietly and meditate or pray.

5) Go and do something else to completely take your mind off of it.

When the designated time period is up, come back to it and then just start writing down the solutions that come to mind, focusing only on solutions.

16

Let Go and Let God

The hardest thing for anyone to do in any situation is to detach, yet it is one of the most important steps in manifesting what you want. Do you have a vision or goal of something that you want? It may be as simple as finding a parking space on a crowded city street, or something bigger, like landing a new client for your business. Perhaps it's getting a date with that special someone, or attaining a large sum of money.

Whatever it is you desire, the process is essentially the same. Create a clear vision of what you want, add as much detail as possible, extract a specific goal from your vision, write it down, and then take whatever action you are inspired to take.

Unfortunately, this is where we generally get off track. It is human nature to want not only to control specifically how it "should" happen, but then to begin obsessing about the fact that it has not yet occurred!

By letting go of the "how" part, you open yourself up to an abundance of possibilities. The Bible advises us to ask for what we want and then believe that we have already received it. Mark 11:24 says, "Therefore I say to you, whatever things you ask when you pray, believe that you receive them, and you will have them." The core message here is ask and believe that it has already occurred.

I am not aware of any teaching that tells us to agonize and obsess until we have what we desire. And I am not aware of any teaching that tells us to sit and worry that it has not yet occurred. Quite the opposite, if you are agonizing or worrying about why you do not already have the results you want, you are, by virtue of your focusing on not yet having it, hindering the blessing or even pushing it away.

If, for example, you want to be in better health and physical condition, create your vision, set some measurable goals, and devise an action plan that will produce the results you are looking for. Then, let go and simply follow your plan. Don't stand in front of the mirror each morning and obsess that you still do not look the way you want. Don't get on a scale every day to see whether or not you are losing excess weight. Just see yourself succeeding and follow your plan. By the grace of God and through the power of your mind, you will be inspired to take certain actions or will be guided to new resources to help you achieve your goal. Relax, let go, and enjoy the journey!

The most successful business people I know have mastered the art of detachment. They create the vision of how their business will be when it's at its peak, set their long- and short-term goals, and develop specific action plans for achieving them.

Then they follow their instincts and stay alert, while taking the appropriate actions.

17

SOMETIMES YOU JUST
NEED TO TRUST

The end of the month was quickly approaching, and like many self-employed people, we were experiencing a cash flow challenge. It was, in all honesty, one of the greatest tests of faith I had experienced in a very long time.

Interestingly enough, I stayed positive throughout, knowing that somehow it would all work out for the best. During the last part of the month my resolve was tested several times. Using everything I have learned about producing the results I desire, I managed to stay in a positive state of mind.

The tricky part, and where I believe many people get tripped up, is holding your attention on what you want, while ignoring the "reality" of what is, and being careful not to dwell upon what hasn't happened yet. Let me explain.

When facing challenging times, a drop in revenue for example, most people devote a lot of time and energy noticing the lack of revenue. This is generally the opposite of what they want. Remember we tend to get more of that which we focus on. The subtlety here is that if we are focusing too much on the lack of revenue, we are more likely to get more lack. The challenge, and I believe the real test of one's faith, is to avoid focusing upon reality and to only focus upon what we want. We then let go and trust that it will appear in the perfect way, in the perfect time.

During my recent challenge, I knew deep within my being that everything would work out. I went about my business, taking appropriate actions, holding my attention on what I wanted, being appreciative for everything I already have, counting my blessings, and *not* focusing upon realty.

A few days before the end of the month, in the middle of a phone call with a friend, I went online to check my bank balance. When I looked at the screen I almost fell over, because what I saw there was a very large deposit in my business account. I rejoiced in what could only be described as a miracle. I realized right then and there that all of our positive focus and refusal to accept lack had, in fact, produced a positive result.

If I have ever questioned the validity of the teachings about the power of our minds, and the law that we tend to get what we focus our lives upon, that moment ended it.

Action Step: Becoming Clear About What You Want.

In your journal complete the steps below.

Step 1) Know what you don't want and write it down.

Step 2) Know what you do want and write it down. Then, spend some time each day getting into the feeling of already having what you desire.

For example, if what you want is more money, you probably don't want little pieces of paper. You probably want a feeling that you associate with having money.

Maybe it's joy, freedom, security, or some other good feeling. Focus on this feeling and recreate it in your body. Imagine you already have the money and are feeling the feelings it brings.

Experience all of the good feelings that will come with your desires. Give no attention to the fact that you do not yet have it. Ignore reality during this "feel good" time. Do this simple exercise for a few minutes each day and you will soon begin to see wonderful results.

18

Don't Focus on Reality

Not focusing on reality may seem like a strange suggestion but that's precisely what we have to do to create change in our lives. It's really quite simple but can be subtly deceptive.

For example, it is pretty much accepted in psychology that we tend to get what we focus on. Or, to put it another way, our minds move in the direction of our thoughts.

Taking that a step further, it becomes apparent that, in order for our lives to change, we must be focusing not on what is, but rather on what we want: in other words, *don't focus on reality*. We must start telling a different story about how our life is.

So many people cling to their "story" about why their life is the way it is and then wonder why it's not changing. It can't!

As long as you're constantly reinforcing conditions as they are, they cannot change. Only when you are willing to let go of your "story" and start telling yourself a new one, will things on the outside begin to change.

If, for example, you want to drop ten pounds, you cannot talk about how hard it is to lose weight or how overweight you are. You cannot keep looking at how slowly the weight is dropping, if at all.

Instead you have to affirm that you are, in fact, losing the weight, and shift your self-talk to that of having already reached your ideal weight. Visualize yourself as already having completed the process.

Affirm, "I am in the process of reaching my ideal (weight, income, lifestyle, or whatever)."

Most people focus their attention on what's wrong, how much they're losing in the market, how they can't pay their bills, and how bad things are in general. The problem here is that they are still holding their attention on the problems. All that can possibly produce are similar conditions; namely, problems.

The only way to change this is to continually focus on and be thankful for the abundance you already have, and you will begin to get more abundance into your life.

You may have to act as though everything is getting better. You have to start acting *as if* you are living the life you desire. Start telling yourself how great it is having the body you want, the income you desire, or the great relationship you've been wanting.

Just doing this for a few minutes a day will cause your mind to eventually believe it is true, and you will soon start to see evidence of your new life showing up. Pay attention to even the slightest sign of your dreams manifesting. If you're affirming an increase in finances and someone buys you lunch, see that as evidence of your new abundance.

This, by the way, is what President Roosevelt did during the depression of the 1930s, and as a result, conditions began changing.

Roosevelt called to the White House the leading positive thinkers of his time, Napoleon Hill, Norman Vincent Peale, etc., and everyone agreed, with the help of the media, to start telling a story of economic recovery.

As people started hearing how things were getting better, they began repeating it and believing it, and, sure enough, things did get better. Everything begins with thought and manifests according to our beliefs.

The quickest way I know of creating positive change in one's life is to start making "appreciation" or "gratitude" lists each day. By putting your attention on what you appreciate and are grateful for in your life, you put yourself in the position to receive more things to appreciate. These, of course, are things you want.

If you doubt what I'm saying, just try it for a few weeks and see what happens. I know from personal experience that your life will begin to improve.

19

ASK BIGGER QUESTIONS FOR GREATER RESULTS

It doesn't get any simpler than that. As with most real wisdom, this idea is very simple to understand and even simpler to implement. If you want a bigger outcome, ask a bigger question. If you want a "better" outcome, ask a "better" question.

What about using questions to get a greater result? For example, let's suppose you own your own business, as I sincerely hope you do. Even a part-time business will not only give you extra income but, more importantly, will give you added peace of mind since you will feel more in control of your income. This can be an important distinction in our current uncertain job market. By the way, you can expect the uncertainty in employment to continue as more and more companies tighten their corporate belts and view people as a resource to be used on an as-needed basis, rather than someone to hire for lifetime employment.

So you have your business, the economy is a little slow, and you want to increase your revenue. You've calculated that five new clients or customers would make up the difference in business and income, so you've been asking yourself, either formally or informally, "How can I attract five new customers?"

As soon as you ask yourself a question, your conscious and subconscious minds go to work coming up with the answers, and you are given new ideas that are in alignment with your question. You will begin thinking of ways to attract the five new customers that you want. Now, what if you were to ask, "How can I attract *fifty* new customers?" You guessed it. Your mind will immediately go to work coming up with ideas for you to attract fifty new customers. How would that feel?

What new, empowering questions could you formulate to help propel you toward your goals?

20

DON'T KILL THE SEEDLINGS

There is a tendency we all have to set a goal to attain something we want, maybe even write it in our journal, and then immediately start undoing it with our own negative self-talk.

How many times have you said, "I want (fill in the blank)," and before your unconscious mind has a chance to assimilate it, you blurt, "But how am I ever going to do that?" Maybe you've said, "I want to date so and so," and then immediately told yourself he or she probably doesn't want to go out with you, so why bother asking.

In many cases, we ask for what we want and then sabotage ourselves with doubts. For example, we might say, "I'd like two new clients." So far, so good. Spending some time each day thinking about that and experiencing what it would feel like to have accomplished it will begin the process of manifesting it in your life.

You will soon find you are having "inspiration" as to ways that you can accomplish this. However, what usually happens is that before the desire can be imprinted on your unconscious mind, you begin to doubt and say things like, "But how am I ever going to do that? I don't have any money for advertising."

This is the "gas/brake" effect. It's like getting into your car, starting the engine, saying "I'm going for a drive in the country," putting the car in drive, stepping on the gas and before you begin to get out of your driveway, slamming on the brake. Obviously, you'll go nowhere. While your desire fired your motivation, your doubts instantly canceled it out. Learn to simply focus on what you want and let go of how you will achieve it.

21

ARE YOU ACTING IN ALIGNMENT WITH WHAT YOU WANT?

If you want to accomplish or receive something, make sure your actions or your talk do not contradict the very thing you are asking for. This is one of those ideas that seems obvious on the surface, but when explored deeper is quite profound.

How many of us experience a desire and then act out of alignment with what we say that we want? For example, are you one of those people who, while you desire more wealth, say things like, "I can't afford that!" Saying things that are not in alignment with what you desire could prevent you from receiving those very things.

Remember we attract what we think about and speak about. If you go through life looking at things that you like and saying "I can't afford that," you never will.

Do you desire health but look in the mirror every day and notice how overweight you are? Again, you cannot attract what you want by noticing what you do not want. The more you notice being overweight, the harder it will be to lose the weight and become healthier.

Instead, when you look in the mirror, notice those things that you *do* like about yourself and are proud of. Start affirming that you are becoming more and more fit each day. Start seeing yourself at your ideal weight. Also, it is obviously not just enough to visualize good results. In addition to thinking and speaking in a positive fashion, you will need to eventually get on the road to eating better and exercising in order to lose weight and become healthier.

Do you want a loving, passionate relationship, but spend your days noticing all the things about your partner that bother you? As the line in the TV commercial once said, "You can't get there from here." Start noticing what you *do* like and appreciate about your loved one, and watch your relationship change.

Remember the principle of "getting what you focus on" is at work in your life, so you should be careful how you judge others. If you say you want one thing, but then behave in a manner that is out of alignment with that, your contradictory behavior will hinder you from receiving or accomplishing what you desire.

Your job is to keep your point of focus on what you want. The more you do this, the more you will see your vision taking hold, and the more your life will change for the better.

A key principle here is to keep reaching for the thoughts that will improve your life for the better and make you feel better. Spend more time thinking about and affirming what you *do* want and less time—or no time at all—focused on what you *don't* want or don't yet have. Your vision will manifest. Just hold true to your desires.

22

LEARN TO VISUALIZE

Whatever you can vividly imagine, you are often more capable of achieving. Everything in your world and everything around you was once an idea in the mind of its inventor or creator.

Invest time each day visualizing what you want in your life. Sit quietly in a place where you will not be disturbed. The best time to do this is just before going to sleep at night and just upon awakening in the morning.

Close your eyes and take a few deep breaths. Relax. Become quiet and at peace.

Mentally create a picture of what you want. See it as vividly as you can. Don't strain. Add color and sound and smells. Engage all of your senses.

You may even want to picture a movie screen in your mind's eye and project your image onto the screen. Just relax and see this picture. Don't worry if it's not a perfect picture. What matters is that you are teaching your subconscious mind what you want to have in your life.

If you want to lose weight and be in better health, see yourself as the person you want to become. If you want a new house, picture it in your mind's eye. See the rooms and property.

What does the kitchen look like? How about the master bedroom? What is the view from the living room window? What about the den? Add as much detail as you can.

After a few minutes of this, say to yourself, "all of this

and more is mine by faith," or some other closing prayer or affirmation.

Doing this for ten or fifteen minutes each day will help you stay on track and will bring into play the power of your thoughts to help you reach your goal.

Relax and have fun with it. Remember the story of the opening day of Walt Disney World in Orlando, when the reporter exclaimed to Walt's nephew, Roy, "It's too bad Walt didn't live to see this." Roy, without missing a beat said, "Walt saw it first; that's why you're seeing it now."

23

TAKE INSPIRED ACTION

After you have put yourself mentally in the place of having what you want, ask for guidance. For example, in the case of starting your own business, you might ask: "What can I do next to build my successful home-based business?" Or, in the case of an exercise program, "What action could I take, right now, to get in shape, reach my ideal weight, and enjoy the process?"

You will notice that you are receiving ideas you may not have considered before. This is because you have first created the vision of what you want and put your energy in alignment with having it. From this point of attraction, you are receiving "inspired action" as opposed to what I call "gerbil action." The latter is what most people are doing. They believe that if they just take enough action, they'll get the result they want. While this may eventually work, it's a much harder way to go about it.

Jot down whatever pops into your mind. Even if an idea seems absurd, write it down anyway. This simple technique has been used successfully by some of the greatest achievers throughout history. People like Thomas Edison, Andrew Carnegie and Henry Ford used this simple technique. They called it, "sitting for ideas." Whatever you choose to call it, it is well worth the time you spend doing it.

Don't Give Up

Don't quit. Just sit for your allotted time period and let your subconscious mind feed you ideas. You may have a thought pop into your consciousness and you will surely uncover creative ways to accomplish your goal. If you do this simple exercise for thirty days, you'll have an arsenal of creative ideas from which to draw and you'll be on your way to attracting your most cherished goal.

The order in which you do this is important. First, see yourself as already being in possession of your desire, affirming that it is yours. Then, and only then, ask what "next action" you can take to bring it to you.

By the way, never ask "how" you are going to achieve a goal. Asking how causes your brain to shift to its logical, analytical left hemisphere, which will return an answer of "I don't know how." Hint: if you knew how, you'd already have what you want.

On the other hand, asking "what" engages your right brain hemisphere which is visual, spatial, and intuitive. This is a much better frame of mind for tasks like brainstorming and encouraging creativity.

24

CHOOSE YOUR
THOUGHTS CAREFULLY

You've probably heard the idea that "Thoughts are things" at one time or another. You've probably nodded your head in agreement, understanding that thoughts are, in fact, things. You probably believe this and accept that your thoughts, being things, do in fact have power.

However, have you really thought about this? Do you apply this to your day-to-day life? Hopefully you do, because your every thought and word is contributing to your life experience.

Your thoughts produce your emotions, which, in turn, result in how you feel about a particular event occurring in your life. It has always amazed me how people can walk around feeling a particular way and not understand that it is their own thoughts, or more accurately, what they are telling themselves, that is producing the feeling in the first place. This is why two people can look at the exact same event and have opposite feelings about it.

You are creating your own reality, moment by moment, with the thoughts you choose to think and the words you choose to say, both to yourself and others.

Let's suppose for a moment that you awaken and immediately start thinking about all of your troubles. This, by the way, is what the majority of people do on a daily basis. At that particular moment in time, your personal experience is negative.

By virtue of the principles of focus, you will seem to get more things to be negative about. The universal laws are based on a specific set of principles that do not waver. People who are critical, for example, will always seem to get more things to be critical of.

The good news is that the opposite is also true. If, for example, you are feeling great, having invested time sitting and reading your goals, and taking time to set your intentions for the day ahead, you are in a place to generally get the things that you want to have in your life.

This is why it is so important to devote time each day, preferably the first thing in the morning and/or the last thing at night, to visualizing your ideal life as though it has already occurred.

25

ENVISION THE LIFE YOU WANT

A recent article in a business magazine posed the question, "If the economy is doing so well, why does everyone feel so bad?"

There are a lot of very sophisticated answers to this question, like "jobs are moving out of the country; there is fear in the world; the cost of living is rising," and so on. I feel that there is one simple reason that is more responsible for people's bad feelings than everything else combined.

You've probably guessed it by now. It's our *attitudes*, which are controlled largely by what we focus upon and what we tell ourselves. We think a thought, which produces a feeling, which leads to an action, which produces a result. It all starts with the thought we choose to think. Attitude is everything.

What else are you focused upon? Do you regularly engage in conversations about how bad things are, or are you looking for what is right and what is working in every situation? The former will increase your bad feelings and take you further in that direction, while the latter will open your awareness to the good that already surrounds you.

While so many people are caught up in talking about everything that is wrong in their world, thereby causing them to feel bad, you can choose the opposite. You can choose to increase the good in your life by focusing your attention and conversation on the good that's already there. To paraphrase the Bible, "To him who has, more is given."

One day, I was feeling "less than great." I began writing

a few things in my journal. I had not written more than three things in total. As I said I was not having a great day.

Then, a very interesting thing happened. By midday I was able to add a couple more things that were working, and by the close of business that day, my list had grown to three times its original length. By shifting my focus, I was once again in a state of mind to receive more of the good things I desired.

Are you willing to create opportunities to receive more of what you want by focusing your attention, and thereby your perception, on what you want? It's your choice how you experience your world. You get to decide what you want to create in your life.

26

Sometimes You Have to Fake It Until You Make It

There is a technique called "fake it until you make it" that works well. I am not suggesting you live in denial, just that you begin to see yourself succeeding. Visualize your successes. See yourself vividly in your mind's eye making the sale and reaching your goals. Affirm over and over that you are succeeding. Write your affirmations daily. Of course, make sure you take the appropriate action, too. Remember, "Faith without works is dead."

Remember that your subconscious mind does not know the difference between real and imaginary. Before you go on a sales call, take a moment and mentally rehearse the scene, just like actors and athletes do. Tell yourself, "I'm a great salesperson." Do this over and over. See the sale being made. See and feel the success. You will be pleasantly amazed at the result. Don't take my word for it. Give it a try. You have nothing to lose and everything to gain.

It has been said throughout history that whatever you believe with conviction, you can achieve. Don't be like the poor elephant and go through your life stuck because of a limiting belief you were given or developed years ago. Break free of the ropes that are holding you back. Take charge of your life and live it to the fullest. You deserve the best.

27

WHAT ARE THE OBSTACLES TO YOUR SUCCESS?

Do you find yourself saying things like "If only I had such and such, then I could follow my dreams?" Do you have a dream that is really burning inside you, but you think you can't do it because of some insurmountable obstacle in your path? Whose obstacle is it? Did you create the obstacle in your mind, or did someone else put it there? How real is it?

In my coaching practice I consistently notice clients erecting obstacles between themselves and their dreams. Interestingly enough, the obstacle is usually in the person's own mind and not really the obstacle that they think it is. Very often it's not even theirs but was put there by some well-intentioned friend or family member. Once we remove the wall, the person is on their way to living their dream.

One way that you can begin to remove the roadblocks to your success is to use a powerful question. For example, you could ask yourself something like, "What is the next step to accomplishing what I want?"

Often we erect these huge walls that limit our progress and keep us from our dreams. By using a different question, like the one above, we can uncover alternative methods to accomplish our goals, become unstuck, and move toward what we desire.

Action Step: Creating the Life of Your Dreams.

If you want to move toward creating the life of your dreams, complete the following exercise:

- What obstacle is standing in my way?

- Is it real?

- If so, what else could I do to move in the direction of my dreams?

- How could I begin right now? Is there someone who can help? (Remember, you do not have to do everything yourself.)

By answering these and other questions you've created, you'll be well on your way to removing the obstacles that are keeping you from realizing your dreams.

28

WHO'S RESPONSIBLE FOR YOUR LIFE?

Taking responsibility actually empowers us to direct our lives rather than be victims of circumstance. If you are abusing your body, yet blaming your poor health on genetics, you are stuck living, as Henry David Thoreau said, "a life of quiet desperation." If you are living below your potential because of something someone else is doing, you are a victim and doomed to a life of disappointment.

If, on the other hand, you take responsibility for all the conditions in your life, the desirable and not so desirable, you are then in a position to change them.

It is important to realize that whether you take responsibility or not, you are always accountable for everything in your life. Whatever the cause of your circumstance, you are living with it, so why not be "driving the bus?" You might as well take ownership of your life and gain the power to change those things that are within your power to change.

In each key area of your life—health, spirituality, business, social, relationships and money—choose one thing that you would like to change. Be sure that it is something within your control. I may want to change the cold winters in Pennsylvania; however, if I want to continue living here, I need to learn to accept them. Of course a good compromise might be to take a winter vacation to a warmer climate.

Assuming it is something that can be changed, ask if it's something you can do or if you need additional assistance. For example, maybe you would like to earn more money and decide that owning your own part-time business is the best way to accomplish this. However, you do not know where to begin. In this case you may wish to speak with a friend who already has a business and learn more about getting started.

If it is something you can change, what are the steps you need to take to accomplish it? Most of the things we would like to change in our lives are well within the scope of our ability to do so, either alone or with help. It is unlikely that you will really want to change things that, like the weather, are totally out of your control. Even if it is something huge, like ending poverty or curing a disease, there are always small steps that you can take. The more you take responsibility for all the conditions and circumstances in your life, the happier you will feel.

By getting actively involved and being honest with yourself, you can determine the quality of life you and your family experience.

If you take the time to get involved with your life, you can gain much greater control of your own destiny.

The next step is action. Get involved. Go out and do something. Get in the game of life. You'll be glad you did.

29

WHAT IF YOU DIDN'T REACH YOUR GOALS?

Something a lot of people don't address, probably because they don't want to appear negative, is what happens when you do not achieve one or more of the goals you set out to accomplish.

There will be times when, no matter how focused you are on a goal, circumstances occur that distract you from your intended objective. When you find yourself in this situation, what can you do?

First, make sure it's your goal and not something you've written down because it sounds good, or you feel it'll impress your friends. Make sure that you are not trying to live out someone else's goals, either.

Is there a reason why you have not achieved the goal? Did more important obligations require your time and energy? Was your goal too far out of reach in the first place? Do you really believe you can achieve it, or is something blocking you? While goals do not need to be "realistic," they do need to be believable to your own mind.

Do you have the knowledge and information needed to reach your goal? For example, I've spoken with many authors who want a best-selling book, but have no idea what it takes to achieve this.

If you have a true *desire* to achieve your goal, have amassed the knowledge and information that you need, have a strong *belief* you will achieve it, and are taking *daily actions* towards your desires, be patient.

Trust in divine timing and know that if you have not yet reached your goal, it's probably because there is something even better coming your way. Remember that things happen in God's time, not ours. Just move your target date forward and keep moving in the direction of your dreams. Your greatest success may be just around the corner.

30

MONEY IS A MEASURE OF YOUR SERVICE

If you want more money, give more service. Where are you serving? Are you delivering your very best, or are you one of those people who can't understand why they never get a raise, even though they do as little as possible?

I was fortunate that at a very young age I was taught to give my very best no matter what the task or job.

One of my first jobs as a teenager was working as the busboy at a family restaurant. On my first day, I was given the task of keeping the patio eating area clean. Because of the values instilled in me by my family and my natural desire to be good at whatever I did, I tackled the job with all the enthusiasm of a CEO about to launch a new division.

The place sparkled. By the third day, the management and customers could easily see the difference. Coincidentally, it was not long before I turned in my mop and pail for a waiter's jacket and then, soon after that, I was training as a cook.

Whether you work for a company or are an independent businessperson dealing with your own clients, make a habit of delivering the very best service you are capable of delivering.

Go the extra mile in everything you do. This is a characteristic that business expert Andrew Carnegie, one of the wealthiest and most successful men of his time, considered to be one of the seventeen traits for a successful life. You will soon see your career or business flourishing, and watch as your income follows.

31

What Do You Believe About Wealth?

What are your beliefs about wealth or about how much money you can have? What about wealthy people? Are they just like you? Or is wealth reserved for some other "special" person?

For example, did you receive messages growing up, like I did, that rich people were those "other people" and not like our friends or us?

Or did you have wealthy friends and family in your life?

Chances are your early money experiences set the stage for your current beliefs about the subject of wealth and how it relates to you.

If you want to be financially comfortable, even wealthy, maybe even rich, you have to begin creating positive associations about the idea. You need to begin seeing yourself as "one of those rich people" before you can become one.

The secrets of achieving anything in life are always "be, do, have."

First, in your mind, "be" the wealthy, successful person you want to become.

Then "do" the things that person would do.

You will then "have" what you want.

Most people get it backwards. They think after they have money, then they'll do good things and they'll be the kind of person they want to be. It does not work that way. First *be*, then *do*, you will then *have*. By the way, this applies to any condition you want to create.

Action Steps

What kind of person would you be if you had that wealth you want?

What are some of the things that person would do?

32

WHERE ARE YOU STARTING FROM?

What is your present income? Again, keep in mind that where you are starting from is not all that important; it's knowing your reference point. There are people who teach that you "should" set an income goal that is no more than 10 percent over where you are now.

I do not agree with this. I have exceeded this and have seen countless others do the same. It's all a matter of your belief about what is possible.

We'll go into that in more detail later; but for now, just get a sense of the gap between where you are presently and where you want to be.

What is your present income?

What income level would you like to be at in one or two years?

Take some time and ask yourself what your life would look like if your finances were ideal. How would you feel if you had as much money as you wanted? What is your ideal vision for your life?

Like the traveler, you will have a very difficult time arriving at your destination if you don't know where it is. As the Cheshire Cat said to Alice in *Alice in Wonderland*, "If you don't know where you're going, any road will take you there."

Start thinking about what you want financially and in your relationships with the money in your life. Begin seeing your life the way you want it to be.

33

THE TWO WAYS TO FINANCIAL FREEDOM

If you want to live better financially and have more of what money can buy, things like freedom and great experiences, there is only one way to do it. This is the part you may not want to hear.

Earn more.

Spend less!

It's important that you pay attention to both. I'm not suggesting that you skimp and deprive yourself of the good things life has to offer. Life is too short to live that way. This is where I disagree with Suze Orman, as much as I admire what she has done to teach people about finance.

I like eating in great restaurants, traveling first class, driving a luxury car, wearing nice clothes, and living well, so my plan has always focused on increasing my income to be able to afford the lifestyle I want to live.

Of course, I also believe in cutting expenses where I can, as long as I can do it without compromising my lifestyle.

Even if you're in a salaried job or have a fixed income, there are hundreds of ways you can increase your income. Just look around you. What can you add to the world that people will pay you for? What skills or talents do you have that could be transformed into even a part-time income? What specialized knowledge do you possess that others will pay to learn about? These are just some of the ways you can free yourself from worrying about rising prices causing hardship for your family.

34

CHANGE THOSE THINGS YOU CAN CHANGE

L et's face it; the price of most things is pretty much out of our control.

Is it right? Is it fair? Of course not, but it is what it is. Like someone once said, "Expecting life to always treat you fairly just because you're a good person is like expecting a bull not to charge you because you're a vegetarian."

What we *can* change is the effect that these things have on our families and on us. We can stop being victims, reclaim our personal power, and take charge of our own destinies.

Is this easy? No, it's not. But it is essential in order to feel in control of our lives, which in turn, affects our happiness.

It requires developing a belief in ourselves and our ability to control our income, regardless of the outside circumstances. It requires us to stop complaining about what we have no control over. It's true that prices are rising. I cannot change that.

I can, however, change whether or not this causes my loved ones and me a hardship. What about people on fixed incomes? Don't they deserve a break? Of course they do, but it isn't happening.

If you're on a fixed income, salary, or pension, you'd better find ways to increase your income or get used to doing without. This is sad but true.

Personally, I've "gone without" enough in my life to not want to live that way as I get older. I've chosen to take control of my income and not be a victim to the whims of the government or big business.

I've delivered seminars to a lot of different types of people, including those at the lower end of the socioeconomic scale. Since I've been there myself, I can empathize with them.

One of the problems a lot of these people have is that they see their circumstance as being outside of themselves. They develop a "them against me" mindset. While this may or may not be accurate, it leaves them powerless to change the situation until "they" change.

These people are stuck right where they are unless they are willing to take full responsibility for the conditions in their lives. Then, and only then, do they have the power to change.

If I am in a situation because of something the government, my company, my spouse, or anyone else is doing, I am stuck there until *they* change. In the case of governments and corporations, this is very unlikely to happen.

However—and here is the big "ah ha"—once I take responsibility, I have the power to do something about it. I'm back in control of my own life. Whatever your circumstances, you can change them . . . if you're willing to own them.

In most of the world there are endless opportunities for increasing your income. The Internet alone has provided countless ways for people to build their financial stability.

I know a young man in Asia who earned a significant sum of money in just two months from a simple idea for an e-book.

So the big question is, "Are you going to sit on your rear end and whine about the price of things as you struggle to get by? Or are you going to do something to change your own situation?"

35

DO YOU REALLY WANT TO BE RICH?

B efore you answer, think about this. Just because you think
you "should" answer yes, it does not mean it's what you
really want.

Most people want to be financially comfortable and happy.
Rich is an entirely different condition and is not for everyone.

You can choose where you want to play the game, but
before you jump onto the "Let's get rich" bandwagon, think
about the cost of achieving massive wealth and ask yourself if
this is what you really want.

Whether you want millions or a few hundred or thousand
dollars more each month, you can achieve it.

Pick your spot, and later, we'll talk about creating a plan to
get you there.

How Much Is Enough?

Before embarking on any personal development program, it's
a good idea to take some time and think about what your own
personal reference for success is.

In the case of wealth creation, ask yourself what amount
of income—daily, weekly, monthly, annually—will get you
excited.

What level of income will give you a jolt?

Depending upon where you're starting from, this number
will be vastly different.

For someone who is used to a steady income of $25,000 a year, the idea of making $100,000 might do it. However, if you've been regularly earning $90,000 a year, the jump to $100,000 isn't such a big deal.

What is your "magic" number?

Write it in your journal as your "intention."

Intentions are powerful. They send the message that you INTEND to achieve this. Remember, words have power.

You might write something like this:

"I intend that I easily and effortlessly earn $_____ in income each year. (Or each week, each month, etc.)

In our next lesson, we'll look at your present income and gain a sense of the size of the gap between where you are and where you want to be.

Keep in mind that this is only a reference. There is nothing that says you can't go from living below the poverty line to being a millionaire in a short time. People have done it over and over again.

If . . . this is what you truly want.

36

HOW MANY CHANNELS
DO YOU HAVE?

When I was growing up in New York City, we had seven television channels, which at the time seemed quite sufficient.

When I lived in Chico, California, and could not afford cable TV, I was only able to receive one channel. This was, to say the least, very limiting.

Now, with digital cable, we have more channels than I know what to do with, including one showing the same shows I watched as a child.

In thinking about this, I realized this is a great metaphor for the way some people approach their finances.

Are you, like I was in Chico, limited to only one channel of income in your life? Most people are. Most of society receives their income from only one channel—their job. In the case of independent business owners, it's often one big client or one marketing channel.

While this may be accepted as "normal," it can be quite devastating. What would you do if, when you went to work tomorrow, you were told that your job no longer existed? By now, we've all learned how easily this can occur. Companies downsize or even go out of business altogether. Mergers often make people redundant and many a small business has failed because of the failure of their one large client.

I'd like to suggest you consider, if you haven't already, having more than one channel of income.

I'm intentionally using the phrase "channel of income" rather than "source of income," because I believe God is the Source of my supply. However, I can receive this supply through an unlimited number of different channels.

Regardless of your present situation, you can easily add one or more channels of income to not only increase your overall financial health, but to provide you with added security and peace of mind. With several channels of income flowing into your life, if one area slows down for a period, you still have other channels flowing.

37

HOW DO YOU SPEND YOUR MOST CREATIVE TIME?

There is a time when we are most creative, productive, and powerful. A time when we have complete access to all of our resources and can solve virtually any problem.

A time when the great inventors of our time talk about having had their "ah ha" ideas and where many of our most pressing problems have been solved.

It is that time in our lives when we have total access to our power and can tap into the Source of "All That Is" for help with anything in our lives.

The time that I am referring to is our dream time, those precious hours just after we drift off to sleep. This is some of the most creative time that we have available to us.

Unfortunately, most people prepare themselves for entering this time by watching late night news programs just before retiring for the night. While I have nothing against TV news programs and even worked in network television years ago, I am totally against watching news just before you go to bed.

This is the absolute worst thing you can do. Think about the imagery that you are taking with you into your dream state: vivid images of war, murder, tragedy, and mayhem of every kind. This is what people are giving their subconscious mind to work with during the time of their most heightened productivity.

It's no wonder so many people are unhappy and depressed. How could you not be?

For those of you who have a habit of watching late night news, I will challenge you to an experiment.

For the next thirty days, in place of the late night news, use that time to listen to a self-help audio program or read an inspiring book.

If you do this for just thirty days, I personally guarantee that your life will improve.

By substituting positive, uplifting ideas in place of all the negative ones that you are getting from the TV news, you will be giving your subconscious mind thoughts, words, and images of the kind of life you want to be living.

You will be giving it the fuel to ignite your dreams and it will pay you back by showing you ways to achieve them.

You will be drifting off to sleep with images of your goals and a positive feeling about achieving them. This will have a dramatic effect on your creativity and outcomes. Don't be surprised if you start waking up with new, empowering ideas that will propel you toward even greater success. I'd be surprised if you do not.

These images will provide your subconscious mind with a clear picture of what you want. Since your subconscious acts on whatever commands you give it, it will begin bringing it towards you.

P.S.: If you must watch the news, please do it earlier in the evening so that you are not processing all the negativity during your most productive time. Better yet, don't watch it at all.

38

Take Time to Play

No matter how much you truly love and enjoy your work, it is necessary, from time to time, to get away from it all. This may mean going on a trip, even if only for a day or two, or an extended vacation of several weeks. Perhaps, for some, it means staying right where you are, but taking time away from your day-to-day work to get out and see what's around you.

Believe it or not, doing this can be the best strategy you have, especially if you're in a rut. Removing yourself from the daily routines associated with running your business or household not only helps clear your mind and opens you to new ideas and possibilities, but it will also take you out of your patterned behavior and stimulate your creativity by presenting new experiences, sights, and stimuli.

Being away from your everyday environment gives you the opportunity to see what life is like for other people in other locations. Whenever I travel, I make a point of observing what local businesses are doing. I usually talk to one or two business people in the town or city I'm visiting. This gives me a totally new perspective on things and opens my thinking to new possibilities.

Simply being in an unfamiliar location causes us to think and act differently. It takes us out of our routines, moves us away from our comfort zones, and literally bombards our creative minds with new and exciting sights and sensations.

Take time to play. Not only will you return more relaxed and rested, you'll surely have new ideas and renewed enthusiasm for your life and your work.

39

WHO ARE YOU LETTING IN YOUR SANDBOX?

I was having lunch the other day with a friend who is an attorney. We were talking about being true to your word and how so many people he encounters try to manipulate circumstances by using fancy legal maneuvers.

As I listened—aside from being thankful I do not have to associate with such people—it reminded me of the way children react while playing in the sandbox. If you've ever watched a young child playing, she will get into a sandbox to play with the other children already there. After a while, if the child does not like what is taking place, she will leave and go join another group more to her liking.

Life, and business in particular, are a lot like that. You can choose who you associate with. Even people in difficult situations, like my friend, Jim, can change the types of people they encounter every day if they choose to.

Who's in your sandbox? Whose sandbox are you playing in?

Are you surrounding yourself with people of integrity, who always play so everyone wins? Or are you getting into dealings with people you do not like or trust?

Personally, I have one steadfast rule: If I don't like or trust someone, I am not going to be around them. Some people may argue that in business you have to deal with people that you don't enjoy being around. I disagree. As the title of one of my books echoes, this is my life, not a dress rehearsal. I have no

intention of spending it in the company of people that I do not
enjoy being with.

There are plenty of good, honest, fun, and supportive people with whom I can play. People who are happy to join me
in my sandbox. If you do this, after a while, you will find that
the only people who are showing up in your life are the kind
of people you want to be around. The others don't even come
into your reality.

Action Step:

Who's in your sandbox? Are they the kind of people you want
to be with?

Who would you like to be on your team? What if you got
to know them by offering to help them with something they're
working on?

Make a list of the people you associate with regularly. Next
to each name, place a "star" if they are positive, supportive
people.

Evaluate your list and decide to spend more time with the
people you've identified as the kind of people who are positive
and supportive of your goals. Remember, we become like the
people we most associate with.

Of course, in some cases you cannot eliminate negative
people from your life; however, you can minimize your contact
and interaction with them.

The more you intentionally choose with whom you spend
your time, the more enjoyable your life will become.

40

CHOOSING TO BE HAPPIER

Regardless of the situation, we always choose our thoughts. This is the key to being happier. Remember, "As a man thinketh in his heart, so is he."

Our thoughts determine the pictures we create in our minds, which in turn control our emotions and determine how we feel.

What happens to us is not nearly as important as how we *respond* to what happens. This is why, in any given circumstance, some people are able to maintain their balance, while others, experiencing the exact same thing, become out of control.

You are always in a position of choice over the thoughts you think and what you choose to focus your attention on.

It's true there are always undesirable things happening in our world; however, unless it's something you can control, dwelling on these things is a waste of your time. It's like the people who stop to look at an accident. This does nothing to help anyone. If you can help, by all means, do so. If not, move on.

By choosing higher thoughts, moment-to-moment, you are taking charge of your mental state, which determines your overall happiness.

The way you can apply this in your daily life is, when faced with a situation that may cause you stress, ask yourself what other thought you could choose to think that would make you feel better than the thought you are presently thinking.

Do this, a little at a time, always asking, "What new thought could I now choose that will cause me to feel even better?"

You can use this technique to shift how you feel in any circumstance, regardless of what is happening. By raising your personal vibration, as a result of choosing a higher thought, you will have raised the vibration of your feelings and emotions, which will, in turn, produce more of the results you want to achieve.

41

You're Never Alone

I'll never understand why we, as human beings, constantly think we're controlling the universe; we're not. I realize that our egos are attempting to stay in control, even though we all know it never works that way. All spiritual or religious teaching of the past several thousand years has taught that our role is essentially to ask for what we want, believe it is on its way, and act as if it is occurring by giving thanks for having received it.

That's it! We don't need to figure out how. As a matter of fact, trying to figure out how our dreams will manifest is the biggest roadblock to our success.

I am always amazed at how easily I, and I'm fairly sure many of you, slip back into the habit of trying to figure things out on our own.

Even though we know there is Divine Guidance available to us. Even though we know we are not alone here on this spinning little planet in the middle of the universe. Even though we have learned, over and over through our experiences, that whenever we truly ask for help, whether it is through prayer, meditation, or some other spiritual practice, it has always been there.

I have had experience after experience, from being at the bottom and thinking my life was over, to needing help to solve a business challenge, to something as simple as finding my way when lost on a highway in a strange city.

Each time I sincerely asked for help, it was there. The

phone would ring; I would see something on a sign or in a newspaper; or a friend would make a suggestion. Whatever the situation, there have been many times in my life when the help from above was clearly there for me.

The interesting thing is that the more one looks at these signs, as with everything we focus upon, the more they are there to be seen. I know this has happened to you, too.

One thing is for sure: the more I "let go and let God," the less stress I feel and the easier my life becomes. The more I trust and do my part—which is essentially to identify what I want, making my intentions and desires known, believing I will receive it, and acting on my intuition—the more everything in my life falls into place.

I encourage you to give this a chance to work in your life, if you're not already doing so.

42

SOMETIMES YOU HAVE TO ASK FOR HELP

The other day I was watching a video of the late Og Mandino. It was his last recorded seminar prior to his passing.

I've been a big fan of his for many years and have listened to several of his audio programs and read most of his fourteen books. I especially identified with the fact that he, like me, had been down and out at one time, caught up in the throes of addiction.

Incidentally, what changed his life, and mine, was God's grace, along with reading self-help books and listening to audio personal development programs. I cannot stress the importance of this enough. We become what we think about, and what we think about is the result of what we put into our minds.

In the video, Og tells the story of the life of actress Lillian Roth, played by Susan Hayward in the move *I'll Cry Tomorrow*. She, too, was living in despair, unable to change her life until she uttered three little words, which were the same words I used when I was in despair. These three words were the basis of Mandino's talk, and are also the basis of this chapter.

These three short words, totaling a mere nine letters, are the most powerful words any of us can use to create a shift. They work whether one is suffering from an addiction, as in the case of Ms. Roth, growing a business, losing weight, attracting a relationship or, as is my present case, marketing a new book.

The words, which you may have already guessed, are "I need help!"

How simple is that? Yet how often do you ask for help?

Most of us would rather offer to help a friend than ask that same friend to help us. I'm not sure exactly why this is so. Maybe we don't like to admit needing anyone's help because it makes us vulnerable or may be perceived as a sign of weakness. Women are better at asking for help when they need it; but we men, for the most part, try to appear "macho" and able to handle everything by ourselves.

If you want to get ahead in your life, especially in business, you'll need to ask for help from time to time. We all need help. Success is a team sport.

In their wonderful book, *The Aladdin Factor*, Jack Canfield and Mark Victor Hansen suggest you ask, ask, ask, and keep asking for what you need. This, by the way, is how I obtained Mr. Canfield's endorsement for my first book, *Handbook to a Happier Life*.

What is it you need help with? Who could you ask? (Hint: *everyone*)

Whatever it is you need help with, begin with the people closest to you and branch out from there to include your friends and network. If necessary, ask total strangers. You'd be amazed at how willing people are to help if only they are asked.

Remember, in an abundant universe, we all win!

**"I have come that they may have life, and
that they may have it more abundantly"
(John 10:10).**

43

GO FOR THE COOKIE

Sometimes you've just got to go for the cookie. In our continual striving to do better, feel better, and look better, we sometimes forget that life is supposed to be fun, too.

When was the last time you ordered something at a restaurant just because you wanted it, without feeling guilty that you "shouldn't"? I'm not suggesting that you go out and start making poor food choices based solely upon what your eyes and head want; that would be foolish. I am suggesting, however, that once in a while we throw caution to the wind and eat something that just feels good.

We can apply the same philosophy to virtually any area of our lives. Instead of following your regular exercise program, what would happen if you just went for a leisurely walk?

The emotional nurturing that you would receive from these types of "feel good" activities would surely outweigh any detrimental effect, so why not lighten up a little and have some fun?

The next time you face a choice between a chocolate chip cookie and a bowl of fruit, just go for the cookie and have some guilt-free pleasure.

44

FEELING BETTER WHEN YOU'RE FEELING DOWN

Being thankful and appreciative is one of the keys to living a happier and more successful life. And this is a great way to attract more situations and experiences to feel thankful for. But . . . what if . . . you don't feel particularly thankful right now? What if, like many people, you're having a difficult time and are feeling a bit of self-pity?

How can you change how you feel even when you're feeling down and would rather just sit and feel sorry for yourself?

Let's face it, we've all been there at one time or another and will probably be there again. We've all experienced times when we just did not feel very thankful. I know I have. We have all experienced times when life just seemed to be singling us out for difficulties. What do we do then?

The fastest and most effective way I know to change how you're feeling about yourself is to get out of your own head. Get out of your own problems and concerns. Go out and do something for someone else. I guarantee you will feel better after doing this.

You could do anything from volunteering to help feed the elderly, delivering a bag of groceries to someone in need, donating some of your unwanted clothing, visiting someone in a hospital or nursing home, or any number of other things that will enable you to get out of your own situation long enough for your perspective to change. You'll be amazed how much your "problems" have changed when you're finished.

Following are a couple of other things you can do to make yourself feel better:

- Write a list of everything that is good in your life.

  What's working? What are you grateful for? Be sure to list every little thing you can think of. The more the better. It's a fact that a person cannot feel gratitude and be in self-pity at the same time.

- Refuse to take part in gossip.

  Gossip serves no one. Remember, what you give out comes back. Besides, whom do you think the gossips are talking about when you're not there? If you want to be happier and more at peace, choose not to partake. By the way, this is a great practice for family gatherings.

45

CONSISTENCY IS KEY

One of the most important traits that we must develop if we are to continue to move toward our goals and aspirations is consistency. While this sounds like a pretty simple thing to do, in practice it tends to be elusive, at least to many of us.

Over the years, I've observed both in myself and in my entrepreneurial clients, the tendency towards spurts of activity followed by long periods of inactivity.

At the start of each New Year, many people vow to "make this year different." While this is quite good and admirable, in practice it often leads to disappointment.

Let's take something simple like exercise, for example. January first comes along and most of us vow to begin our exercise program and get back into shape. We may even join a health club or buy some expensive equipment. We have the best of intentions. Unfortunately, within a few months, or even weeks, our old habits return and we find ourselves exercising less and less.

Statistically, health club memberships drop off significantly by March. The question then becomes, "How do we develop the consistency to maintain our commitment over the long term?"

One way, and this may sound overly simple, is to "just do it." A habit can be changed after about thirty days of consistent practice. So if we just "bite the bullet" and do it steadily for a month, we'll greatly increase our chance for success.

Another more powerful method is to get leverage on yourself

by writing, in great detail, everything that you will gain by sticking to your new program, and conversely, everything that it will cost you if you don't. This "carrot and stick" approach, using the leverage of pain and pleasure, is a great motivator in any situation.

Another way is to get a coach, mentor, or buddy who will hold you accountable and help encourage you to stay with your commitment. Of course, this same process can be applied in any area of your life or business.

Consistency in your relationships, business marketing, finances, and personal development is the key to long-term progress and a happier, more fulfilling life.

By the way, a great commitment you can make is to read a personal development or inspirational book for ten to fifteen minutes each day. You will be amazed at what that one simple habit will do for you.

46

CHANGE YOUR ACTIONS, CHANGE YOUR LIFE

The statement above is one of those things that, at first glance, seems obvious; however, if you really think about it, you'll see the wisdom in it.

As a rule, we tend to live our lives pretty much doing the same things over and over. We watch the same TV shows, eat pretty much the same foods, dine at the same restaurants and even tend to dress ourselves the same way each day.

If you remember the television show *All in the Family*, you may remember a skit where Archie, played by Carroll O'Connor, and his son-in-law, played by Rob Reiner, are arguing about whether one should put both socks on before their shoes or put one sock and a shoe and then the other.

This was a funny scene and made for entertaining television. But if you stop and think about it, you probably do one or the other every time you get dressed and have probably been dressing yourself the same way since you were a child. You most likely learned it from your parents.

While something as benign as how you dress yourself will have little, if any, effect on your success, your other habits will.

By changing your habits and altering your patterns, you can improve certain aspects of your life by producing new associations.

Something as simple as changing the route you take to and from work each day will cause you to see new things, which will spark new thoughts and ideas. As a result, you will increase your creativity.

Do you take pretty much the same actions in your work or business each day? Most of us have routines we follow, and while there is nothing wrong with this, it can stifle our creativity and prevent us from major breakthroughs.

What could you do to change your routine? Could you change some of the daily actions you take? For example, would changing the way you handle email enable you to take a new action or complete a more urgent task?

I found myself answering my email first thing in the morning, as though the sender was sitting there at 6 a.m. waiting for my answer. While this is unlikely, it does prevent me from doing something more important.

Scheduling a specific time to answer my email has freed my early morning time for me to write. Not only is this the most important component of my work, it is also the time I write best, since my mind is still clear and calm after my morning meditation and quiet time.

Delaying email further has provided me with the opportunity to get back to my morning exercise, another task that is critical to my well-being.

When I go out, I always follow a different route to wherever I'm going. Over time, I have found this drive time to be one of the best times for brainstorming ideas. I carry a small digital recorder to capture any ideas I have while driving.

The more you can "shake up" your routines, the more you will stimulate your creative mind. If you want to try an interesting experiment, when you're getting dressed in the morning, put your pants on the opposite way from how you usually do it. If you usually place your right leg in first, this time put your left leg in first. Be sure to stand where you can sit quickly, since this may well cause you to lose your balance. That is how strongly we are conditioned to our daily routines.

When you take a shower, wash yourself in a different way than you usually do and notice how strange it feels. Take a new route to work tomorrow and see how that feels. Brush your teeth with your opposite hand and notice how this feels.

The more you take advantage of opportunities to stimulate your mind, the more you will find new, creative ideas popping into your head, and the more likely you will produce significant results. This is where breakthroughs come from.

47

ALLOWING THE ABUNDANCE YOU DESIRE

On a recent teleseminar, one of the things I discussed was how, although most of us would like to experience abundance in our lives, we become conflicted by the mixed messages we receive from society and the media.

We are steadily bombarded with messages telling us that, in order to be happy, we have to be driving a certain type of automobile, look a certain way, wear a particular brand of clothing, and so on. We are told that, in order to be a success, we must earn a certain amount of money.

On the other side of the coin, we are given negative messages about wealth. The news media loves to tell us detailed stories about business leaders who are greedy and going to jail, or the latest antics of some overindulged celebrity.

The problem is that, as we are being fed a not-so-subtle message that rich people are bad, we are told through advertising that in order to be happy, we need to be rich.

With our natural tendency to want to be decent people, it's easy to see why so many people are confused, and often sabotage their best efforts.

How Do We Change This?

We do it, like many things in life, one step at a time. One simple way is to find new references for what wealth represents to you. For example, two of my favorite authors, Jack Canfield and Mark Victor Hansen, tithe a percentage of sales from their hugely successful *Chicken Soup for the Soul* series of books to charity. This is just one great example of sharing the wealth. Personally, I've been tithing for years and, as a result, watched my own success grow.

There are more people doing good with their wealth than there are who don't. These are the "Enlightened Millionaires," as defined by Mark Victor Hansen and Robert G. Allen in *The One Minute Millionaire*. Their definition is a person who comes from abundance, adds massive value, gives back, and leaves a lasting legacy. What more could anyone ask for?

Next, begin to see yourself as a positive, generous, wealthy person. Affirm, "I am wealthy, and I use my wealth for the good of myself and others."

Get used to being around the finer things you'd like to attain in life. For example, if you want a luxury automobile, start getting used to the idea by going to a dealership. There's no charge for walking around the dealer's showroom. As a mater of fact, you can usually get a complimentary cup of coffee there.

If you want to upgrade your wardrobe, begin by spending time shopping in better quality stores. You can buy expensive clothes for less by shopping the "reduced for clearance" racks, outlet stores, or even high-end designer consignment shops. These, by the way, are tricks I learned from my wife, who is a consummate shopper.

Do something luxurious for yourself. It does not need to be expensive. Just take some amount of money, whatever you can afford, and splurge on something nice for yourself. It could be something as simple as a manicure or a massage, or even an ice cream sundae.

For many people, this can be a major breakthrough. My mother, for example, would never consider spending on herself, although she splurged on her children and grandchildren. Does this sound like you?

While it may be "better to give than to receive," it's still pretty nice to receive!

48

GIVING BACK

One of the greatest feelings of personal satisfaction comes from being able to give to others, especially those who are less fortunate. There are many ways you can use your wealth to enrich your neighborhood, your spiritual community, and those who need a helping hand. There is an added payback for you in that, as I wrote earlier, it is virtually impossible to give without receiving.

The practice of tithing is written about in every book on success and spirituality and is a universal law. Tithing a percentage of your income, usually 10 percent, to your church or other spiritual organization not only helps that group but also reinforces your prosperity mindset by declaring that you are wealthy enough to afford to do this.

Many people have the attitude that they will tithe when they, themselves, have more. This is backwards. If you follow the teachings of scripture and great religious teachers throughout history, you will learn that the best time to begin tithing is when you yourself are in need. This opens up the opportunity for you to reap the good that you have sown.

Besides, it's a lot easier to make a habit of tithing if you begin with small amounts. The wealthier you are, the larger the amount of your tithe, and the harder it is to write the check. If you doubt this, imagine how it feels to tithe ten percent of a thousand dollars. Easy enough, right? You just write a $100 check.

Now, imagine tithing the same ten percent but this time

imagine the amount to be one hundred thousand dollars. The check you'd be writing would then be $10,000. Which would you find easier to give away?

It is a universal law that as you give, so shall you receive. Consequently, it is impossible to give unconditionally and not receive. As a matter of fact, you tend to receive more than you give.

The Bible talks about receiving thirtyfold (and more), so you cannot lose. This is an amazing principle, and one that anyone, regardless of their situation in life, can employ.

You can always give something—love, time, money, labor, and material goods. Even an act of simply giving a little of your time to help another will bring you untold rewards.

I'm not talking about giving with the wrong type of expectation or motivation, or doing good deeds solely for personal gain or selfish ambition. I'm suggesting that you can give freely of yourself, your money, and your time, knowing that whatever you give will be returned to you in some way.

Giving and helping one another are some of the most rewarding things we can do. Giving returns to us a sense of personal satisfaction and good feelings that money cannot buy. It is our nature to give and to serve. We are here to give and to help each other.

I was once asked if I knew how much money billionaire J. Paul Getty left when he died. When I said I did not know, my friend replied, "All of it."

You see, we are taking nothing with us when we pass away, except our good deeds. To me, this simple fact is proof that we are here to give and to serve. Otherwise, we would be able to take our possessions with us when we die.

49

SEEK TO SERVE

It was many years ago when I was first introduced to the idea that "money is a measure of your service. If you want more money, give more service."

At the time I was a new distributor for a network marketing company, listening to one of the company's leaders. I paid close attention since he was earning more money than I could even imagine at the time.

Too often we ask ourselves, "What can I do to earn more money?" Wrong question. Money is the reward we are given for providing a level of service to the world, whether in the form of a product or by providing some other benefit.

If you want more money ask where you can serve. What can you do either in your business or at your job that would increase the service you are rendering to society, your community, and your employer?

We are on this earth to serve, to give. The fact that we take nothing with us when we leave is proof of that.

If you look around, you will soon realize that the people benefiting most, the people earning the most, are also those who are making the biggest contributions to society.

The movie star who receives a huge sum of money for making a movie is also providing entertainment to the millions of people who pay only a small sum for the entertainment. The athlete, musician, and author are also providing entertainment or other valuable services to millions.

The business owner who is widely successful is most likely

providing a superior product or service. A waiter or waitress in a restaurant who receives the most tips is also probably the one providing the best service.

By remembering the concept that we earn money as a result of our service, you will remember to seek opportunities to serve more whenever you desire an increase in your earnings. Seek to serve, and you will never want for wealth in your life.

50

SUCCESS TO SIGNIFICANCE

A number of years ago I attended a Zig Ziglar seminar with my wife, Georgia. It was awesome. Since we had VIP tickets, we were part of a small group who attended the welcome breakfast with Zig and had the opportunity to talk with him as he greeted people outside the meeting room. As a matter of fact, it was when my first book had just been published. I gave him a copy and later received a lovely letter of encouragement from him.

One of the key principles he spoke about that day was something that you do not hear about very often. That's unfortunate since it is probably the most important key to a happy and fulfilling life.

Let's face it, most of us are already reasonably successful by our own definition, or at least on our way. If you consider Earl Nightingale's definition of success "The progressive realization of a worthy ideal," you're most likely successful right now. So what's next? Is this all there is? Of course not.

There is another step in life's progression that's even more rewarding than achieving high levels of success. It's *significance*. Doing something bigger than you; leaving a lasting legacy. The interesting thing about significant accomplishments is that they are often born of a simple desire to help or do good.

Alexandra "Alex" Scott lived only eight years before cancer took her life. But what a miraculous child. At a very young age, she had the courage and strength to take on her illness and in spite of being very sick, made a difference. She was only four when she decided she wanted to raise funds to help support cancer research.

Beginning with one stand, and with the help of her family, her lemonade stands continue to raise funds to fight cancer. To date, *Alex's Lemonade Stand Foundation* has raised over $25 million for childhood cancer research.

What about you? What causes or issues are important to you? What simple steps might you take, starting now, to begin to do something for a cause that you are passionate about?

If each of us became involved in improving just one human condition, we would soon be living in a much better world.

51

GIVE YOURSELF THE GIFT OF QUIET

The other day I was having coffee with a friend, enjoying a conversation about personal development books and such. When she mentioned the name of a well-known author, a man sitting at the next table chimed in. Before long we were in a three-way conversation on the subject.

Our new acquaintance went on about how much reading self-help books and listening to audio programs had helped him. He explained how he had, at one time, a problem with his temper and how he was always stressed out. "When I started reading these books," he revealed, "I began to relax more and changed my outlook on life."

He then explained how, even though the books and audios were helping, when he started meditating he was able to achieve a sense of calmness he had never before experienced.

As someone who has consistently practiced meditation of one form or another for over twenty years, I can attest to its values. Over the years I've found that when I give myself the gift of time to meditate or even just spend ten or fifteen minutes in quiet, especially first thing in the morning, my day goes more smoothly.

In my first book, *Handbook to a Happier Life*, I wrote about some of the health benefits that include actually slowing the aging process. One study, in England, concluded that each year of regular meditating takes off approximately one year of aging. And it lowers blood pressure and slows our heart rate.

What really matters to me is that I take the time to do it.

While I do not follow a particular system, I do use specially made audios for my times of meditation.

If you were to look at my MP3 device, along with music and a wide variety of personal development and business seminars, you'd see several of these special audio programs which I rotate for my daily meditation practice. While I realize that meditation purists may disagree with my methods, I believe in using the technology that's available to help "get me there." There are many methods of meditation available for you to try. Feel free to explore them to create a routine that works for you. What really matters is that you take the time to do it.

52

CHOOSE INDEPENDENCE

Declare your independence from allowing outside forces to determine how you feel.

Declare your independence from allowing the stock market or other economic indicators to determine your financial health.

Declare your independence from allowing advertisers to determine how you should look and what you should eat.

The only one who can determine the conditions in your life, including how you feel and how much money you have or do not have, is you. You are responsible for your own life, and the sooner you realize this, the sooner you will have the power to change what you want to change.

Your thoughts create your life experience. Whatever you are experiencing in your life right now is the result of the thought patterns you've had in the past, either consciously or unconsciously.

The Bible tells us that "As a man thinketh, so is he." This idea has been repeated by every spiritual teaching for the past 2,000 years or more. It's time we honored it and took back our own personal power. It is time we took back control of our thoughts.

Begin today to take an active role in creating your life. Choose your thoughts intentionally and with care. Monitor your self-talk. Affirm your dreams and goals daily.

CONCLUSION AND NEXT STEPS

A merican philosopher Henry David Thoreau said, "If one advances confidently in the direction of his dreams, and endeavors to live the life which he has imagined, he will meet with a success unexpected in common hours."

You will notice he said advance "confidently," not fearfully. Step out with confidence and a positive expectation.

"Endeavor to live the life you have imagined." Do your best at all times and you will succeed.

Within the pages of this book are some of the many keys that will assist you in your journey toward a successful and happier life. These are the principles used by virtually all successful people.

I suggest you read and reread this book and others like it on a daily basis. It does not need to take a lot of time. Reading for ten or fifteen minutes each day will help you remain in a positive state of mind.

Take time each day to see, feel, and experience your life as you would like it to be. Immerse yourself in this vision of success.

Associate with positive, uplifting people who want you to succeed.

What you choose to accomplish in your life is entirely up to you. Remember that *within you is the power to change your life*.

May you achieve all the success you desire and so richly deserve.

Be well and God bless,

Jim Donovan
Bucks County, Pennsylvania

About the Author

After overcoming personal challenges, which took away everything he held dear and brought him to the depths of despair, Jim Donovan began a process of recovery. Wanting a more successful life, he began studying success, reading and listening to everything he could find, and attending seminars regularly. As he saw his own life improving beyond anything he expected, he felt compelled to share what had helped him, in the hope of helping others.

Jim began writing and working in the field of human performance in 1987. His background and studies include Western & Eastern Philosophy, and many of the teachers of personal development of the past two centuries. He is a committed life-long learner who studies books and audio programs regularly.

Having first applied the techniques and principles he teaches in his own life, he has risen to a position of international respect and recognition as an author and seminar leader.

Jim is a frequent speaker to businesses, trade groups, and associations. His seminars have benefited hundreds of groups, including banks, medical practices, accounting firms, small business groups, chambers of commerce, women-owned businesses, associations, high school faculty, government employees, network marketing companies, high school and college students, and many others.

His seminars inspire audiences to take charge of their lives, provide them with transformational ideas and strategies for their success, and motivate them to create the lives of their dreams.

An internationally acclaimed author, Jim has written best-selling books that are published in twenty-two countries and are read worldwide, including *Handbook to a Happier Life*;

This Is Your Life, Not A Dress Rehearsal; and *Don't Let an Old Person Move Into Your Body.*

Since 1991, Jim has written *Jim's Jems*, his syndicated newsletter for personal and professional development. Jim's articles regularly appear in newspapers, magazines, and on websites. Jim is a popular guest on radio and TV talk shows and a member of the "brain trust" for *The Small Business Advocate* syndicated radio show. You can subscribe to his newsletter and receive a free gift at www.JimDonovan.com.